5/83

To: Brenda

With Love from
all of us.

Dee, Lucille,
Rose Anne + Carol

I found this
book and everyone
wanted to
held get it.
for you.
Love Dee

VICTORIA'S SECRET

BEAUTY
OF
LOVE

BEAUTY

OF

LOVE

VOLUME FOUR

Authorized Purveyors

VICTORIA'S SECRET

N⁰ 10 MARGARET STREET
LONDON W1

She walks in beauty, like the night
   of cloudless climes and starry skies;
And all that's best of dark and bright
   Meet in her aspect and her eyes.

SO OPENS BYRON'S match-less tribute to that most mys-terious, and elusive quality, feminine beauty. Delicate and subtle as beauty may be, it has an intoxicating and fascinating potency. The selection of verse and prose that I have made for this treasury, and the lovely images that accompany them, are their own eloquent testi-mony not only to this lasting power, but also to the infinite variety of feminine beauty, which has held poets and painters in thrall throughout history.

The shy, unconscious grace of Cousin Phillis, the innocent voluptuousness of Tess of the d'Urbervilles, the high-spirited recklessness of George Eliot's Gwendolen or Tennyson's Rosalind – all are equally bewitching. So too are the more sophisticated charms of George Meredith's exquisite heroine, elegant as a fashionplate; of Aurelian Townshend's victorious beauty, merciless and magnificent; of Tennyson's serene, languorous Eleanore; and above all the dark, pagan beauty of Eustacia Vye, fascinating and dangerous in its exoticism.

Every action of these beauties provides fresh opportunities to admire their charms: whether waking or sleeping, playing an instrument or weeping, walking or simply looking, all have the power to enslave. In this power lies not only their charm but also their peril, their ability to strike awe in the heart of the beholder: to inspire, in Rossetti's words, 'terror and mystery'.

Yet ultimately, as all the testaments to beauty in these pages show, beauty remains a magical enigma, but one so fascinating, so alluring, that poets and painters will never cease to try to encapsulate it. For, as Spenser wrote four centuries ago,

The glorious portrait of that Angel's face,
Made to amaze weal men's confused skill,
And this world's worthless glory to embase,
What pen, what pencil, can express her fill?

With Love

O BEAUTY

O Beauty, passing beauty! sweetest Sweet!
  How canst thou let me waste my youth in sighs?
I only ask to sit beside thy feet.
  Thou knowest I dare not look into thine eyes.
Might I but kiss thy hand! I dare not fold
  My arms about thee — scarcely dare to speak.
And nothing seems to me so wild and bold,
  As with one kiss to touch thy blessèd cheek.
Methinks if I should kiss thee, no control
    Within the thrilling brain could keep afloat,
      The subtle spirit. Even while I spoke,
The bare word KISS hath made my inner soul
    To tremble like a lutestring, ere the note
      Hath melted in the silence that it broke.

ALFRED, LORD TENNYSON 1809–92

ℱOR PITY, PRETTY EYES

For pity, pretty eyes, surcease
To give me war, and grant me peace!
Triumphant eyes, why bear you arms
Against a heart that thinks no harms,
A heart already quite appalled,
A heart that yields and is enthralled?

Kill rebels, proudly that resist,
Not those that in true faith persist,
And conquered, serve your deity.
Will you, alas, command me die?
Then die I yours, and death my cross;
But unto you pertains the loss.

THOMAS LODGE 1558?–1625

*L*A GIOCONDA

Historic, sidelong, implicating eyes;
A smile of velvet's lustre on the cheek;
Calm lips the smile leads upward: hand that lies
Glowing and soft, the patience in its rest
Of cruelty that waits and does not seek
For prey; a dusky forehead and a breast
Where twilight touches ripeness amorously:
Behind her, crystal rocks, a sea and skies
Of evanescent blue on cloud and creek;
Landscape that shines suppressive of its zest
For those vicissitudes by which men die.

MICHAEL FIELD 1846–1913

M ADE FOR THIS SOUL

Somewhere beneath the sun,
   These quivering heart-strings prove it,
Somewhere there must be one
   Made for this soul, to move it;
Some one that hides her sweetness
   From neighbours whom she slights,

Nor can attain completeness,
    Nor give her heart its rights;
Some one whom I could court
    With no great change of manner,
Still holding reason's fort,
    Though waving fancy's banner;
A lady, not so queenly
    As to disdain my hand,
Yet born to smile serenely
    Like those that rule the land;
Noble, but not too proud;
    With soft hair simply folded,
And bright face crescent-browed,
    And throat by Muses moulded;
And eyelids lightly falling
    On little glistening seas,
Deep-calm, when gales are brawling,
    Though stirred by every breeze:
Swift voice, like flight of dove
    Through minster arches floating,
With sudden turns, when love
    Gets overnear to doting;
Keen lips, that shape soft sayings
    Like crystals of the snow,
With pretty half-betrayings
    Of things one may not know;
Fair hand, whose touches thrill,
    Like golden rod of wonder,
Which Hermes wields at will
    Spirit and flesh to sunder;
Light foot, to press the stirrup
    In fearlessness and glee,
Or dance, till finches chirrup,
    And stars sink to the sea.

WILLIAM JOHNSON CORY 1823–92

BEAUTY

O, how much more doth beauty beauteous seem
By that sweet ornament which truth doth give!
The rose looks fair, but fairer we it deem
For that sweet odour which doth in it live.
The canker-blooms have full as deep a dye
As the perfumed tincture of the roses,
Hang on such thorns, and play as wantonly
When summer's breath their masked buds discloses:
But, for their virtue only is their show,
They live unwoo'd and unrespected fade;
Die to themselves. Sweet roses do not so;
Of their sweet deaths are sweetest odours made:
   And so of you, beauteous and lovely youth,
   When that shall fade, by verse distills your truth.

WILLIAM SHAKESPEARE 1564–1616

 BEAUTY

Sweet mouth, that send'st a musky-rosed breath;
Fountain of nectar and delightful balm;
Eyes cloudy-clear, smile-frowning, stormy-calm;
Whose every glance darts me a living-death
Brows, bending quaintly your round ebene arks;
Smile, that than Venus sooner Mars besots;
Locks more than golden, curl'd in curious knots,
Where, in close ambush, wanton Cupid lurks;
Grace Angel-like; fair fore-head, smooth, and high;
Pure white, that dimm'st the lilies of the vale;
Vermilion rose, that mak'st Aurora pale:
Rare spirit, to rule this beautious Emperie:
    If in your force, divine effects I view,
    Ah, who can blame me, if I worship you?

JOSHUA SYLVESTER 1563–1618

Eustacia Vye was the raw material of a divinity ... She was in person full-limbed and somewhat heavy; without ruddiness, as without pallor; and soft to the touch as a cloud. To see her hair was to fancy that a whole winter did not contain darkness enough to form its shadow: it closed over her forehead like nightfall extinguishing the western glow ... She had Pagan eyes, full of nocturnal mysteries, and their light, as it came and went, and came again, was partially hampered by their oppressive lids and lashes; and of these the under lid was much fuller than it usually is with English women. This enabled her to indulge in reverie without seeming to do so: she might have been believed capable of sleeping without closing them up. Assuming that the souls of men and women were visible essences, you could fancy the colour of Eustacia's soul to be flame-like. The sparks from it that rose into her dark pupils gave the same impression.

The mouth seemed formed less to speak than to quiver, less to quiver than to kiss. Some might have added, less to kiss than to curl. Viewed sideways, the closing-line of her lips formed, with almost geometric precision, the curve so well known in the arts of design as the cima-recta, or ogee.

Her presence brought memories of such things as Bourbon roses, rubies, and tropical midnights; her moods recalled lotus-eaters and the march in 'Athalie'; her motions, the ebb and flow of the sea; her voice, the viola. In a dim light, and with a slight rearrangement of her hair, her general figure might have stood for that of either of the higher female deities. The new moon behind her head, an old helmet upon it, a diadem of accidental dewdrops round her brow, would have been adjuncts sufficient to strike the note of Artemis, Athena, or Hera respectively, with as close an approximation to the antique as that which passes muster on many respected canvases.

The Return of the Native, THOMAS HARDY 1840–1928

Ask me no more

Ask me no more where Jove bestows,
When June is past, the fading rose;
For in your beauty's orient deep
These flowers, as in their causes, sleep.

Ask me no more whither do stray
The golden atoms of the day!
For in pure love heaven did prepare
Those powders to enrich your hair.

Ask me no more whither doth haste
The nightingale, when May is past;
For in your sweet dividing throat
She winters, and keeps warm her note.

Ask me no more where those stars 'light,
That downwards fall in dead of night;
For in your eyes they sit, and there
Fixed become, as in their sphere.

Ask me no more if east or west
The phœnix builds her spicy nest;
For unto you at last she flies,
And in your fragrant bosom dies.

THOMAS CAREW 1595?–1639?

ROSALIND

My Rosalind, my Rosalind,
My frolic falcon, with bright eyes,
Whose free delight, from any height of rapid flight,
Stoops at all game that wing the skies,
My Rosalind, my Rosalind,
My bright-eyed, wild-eyed falcon, whither,
Careless both of wind and weather,
Whither fly ye, what game spy ye,
Up or down the streaming wind?

The quick lark's closest-caroll'd strains,
The shadow rushing up the sea,
The lightning-flash atween the rains,
The sunlight driving down the lea,
The leaping stream, the very wind,
That will not stay, upon his way,
To stoop the cowslip to the plains,
Is not so clear and bold and free
As you, my falcon Rosalind.

ALFRED, LORD TENNYSON 1809–92

TO LANGUISH IN THY BEAUTY

I stand before thee, Eleänore;
  I see thy beauty gradually unfold,
Daily and hourly, more and more.
I muse, as in a trance, the while
  Slowly, as from a cloud of gold,
Comes out thy deep ambrosial smile.
I muse, as in a trance, whene'er
  The languors of thy love-deep eyes
Float on to me. I would I were
  So tranced, so rapt in ecstasies,
To stand apart, and to adore,
Gazing on thee for evermore,
Serene, imperial Eleänore!

ALFRED, LORD TENNYSON 1809–92

*P*ORTRAIT

The glorious portrait of that Angel's face,
Made to amaze weak men's confused skill,
And this world's worthless glory to embase,
What pen, what pencil, can express her fill?
For, though he colours could devise at will,
And eke his learned hand at pleasure guide,
Lest, trembling, it his workmanship should spill;
Yet many wondrous things there are beside:
The sweet eye-glances, that like arrows glide,
The charming smiles, that rob sense from the heart,
The lovely pleasance, and the lofty pride,
Cannot expressed be by any art.
　A greater craftsman's hand thereto doth need,
　That can express the life of things indeed.

EDMUND SPENSER 1552?–99

IVINELY FAIR

At length I saw a lady within call,
    Stiller than chiselled marble, standing there,
A daughter of the gods, divinely tall,
    And most divinely fair.

Her loveliness with shame and with surprise
    Froze my swift speech: she turning on my face
The starlike sorrows of immortal eyes,
    Spoke slowly in her place.

'I had great beauty: ask thou not my name:
    No one can be more wise than destiny.
Many drew swords and died. Where'er I came
    I brought calamity.'

ALFRED, LORD TENNYSON 1809–92

RED POPPIES

She stood breast high amid the corn,
Clasped by the golden light of morn,
Like the sweetheart of the sun,
Who many a glowing kiss had won.

On her cheek an autumn flush,
Deeply ripened; – such a blush
In the midst of brown was born,
Like red poppies grown with corn.

Round her eyes her tresses fell,
Which were blackest none could tell,
But long lashes veiled a light,
That had else been all too bright.

And her hat, with shady brim,
Made her tressy forehead dim; –
Thus she stood amid the stooks,
Praising God with sweetest looks: –

Sure, I said, heaven did not mean,
Where I reap thou shouldst but glean,
Lay thy sheaf adown and come,
Share my harvest and my home.

THOMAS HOOD 1835–74

ADELINE

Thou art not steep'd in golden languors,
   No tranced summer calm is thine,
     Ever varying Madeline.
   Thro' light and shadow thou dost range,
   Sudden glances, sweet and strange,
Delicious spites and darling angers,
   And airy forms of flitting change.

ALFRED, LORD TENNYSON 1809–92

TOLEN FROM THEE

The forward violet thus did I chide:
Sweet thief, whence didst thou steal thy sweet that smells
If not from my love's breath? The purple pride
Which on thy soft cheek for complexion dwells
In my love's veins thou hast too grossly dyed.
The lily I condemnèd for thy hand,
And buds of marjoram had stol'n thy hair;
The roses fearfully on thorns did stand,
One blushing shame, another white despair;
A third, nor red nor white, had stol'n of both,
And to his robb'ry had annexed thy breath;
But for his theft, in pride of all his growth
A vengeful canker eat him up to death.
　　More flowers I noted, yet I none could see,
　　But sweet or color it had stol'n from thee.

WILLIAM SHAKESPEARE 1564–1616

HE ENCHANTMENT

I did but look and love awhile,
   'Twas but for one half-hour;
Then to resist I had no will,
   And now I have no power.

To sigh and wish is all my ease;
   Sighs which do heat impart
Enough to melt the coldest ice,
   Yet cannot warm your heart.

O would your pity give my heart
   One corner of your breast,
'Twould learn of yours the winning art,
   And quickly steal the rest.

THOMAS OTWAY 1652—85

[33]

PICKING ROSES

They had spent some time wandering desultorily thus, Tess eating in a half-pleased, half-reluctant state whatever d'Urberville offered her. When she could consume no more of the strawberries he filled her little basket with them; and then the two passed round to the rose trees, whence he gathered blossoms and gave her to put in her bosom. She obeyed like one in a dream, and when she could affix no more he himself tucked a bud or two into her hat, and heaped her basket with others in the prodigality of his bounty. At last, looking at his watch, he said, 'Now by the time you have had something to eat, it will be time for you to leave, if you want to catch the carrier to Shaston. Come here, and I'll see what grub I can find.'

Stoke-d'Urberville took her back to the lawn and into the tent, where he left her, soon reappearing with a basket of light luncheon, which he put before her himself. It was evidently the gentleman's wish not to be disturbed in this pleasant *tête-à-tête* by the servantry.

'Do you mind my smoking?' he asked.

'Oh, not at all, sir.'

He watched her pretty and unconscious munching through the skeins of smoke that pervaded the tent, and Tess Durbeyfield did not divine, as she innocently looked down at the roses in her bosom, that there behind the blue narcotic haze was potentially the 'tragic mischief' of her drama – one who stood fair to be the blood-red ray in the spectrum of her young life. She had an attribute which amounted to a disadvantage just now; and it was this that caused Alex d'Urberville's eyes to rivet themselves upon her. It was a luxuriance of aspect, a fulness of growth, which made her appear more of a woman than she really was. She had inherited the feature from her

mother without the quality it denoted. It had troubled her mind occasionally, till her companions had said that it was a fault which time would cure.

Tess of the D'Urbervilles, THOMAS HARDY 1840–1928

An Ode

I intended an Ode,
And it turn'd to a Sonnet
It began *à la mode*,
I intended an Ode;
But Rose cross'd the road
    In her latest new bonnet;
I intended an Ode;
    And it turn'd to a Sonnet.

HENRY AUSTIN DOBSON 1840–1921

$\mathcal{R}$OSE

Rose, what is become of thy delicate hue?
And where is the violet's beautiful blue?
Does aught of its sweetness the blossom beguile,
That meadow, those daisies, why do they not smile?
Ah! rivals, I see what it was that you dressed
And made yourselves fine for; a place in her breast:
You put on your colours to pleasure her eye,
To be plucked by her hand, on her bosom to die.

JOHN BYROM 1692–1763

TO AMARANTHA, THAT SHE WOULD DISHEVEL HER HAIR

Amarantha sweet and fair,
Ah, braid no more that shining hair!
As my curious hand or eye
Hovering round thee, let it fly!

Let it fly as unconfined
As its calm ravisher the wind,
Who hath left his darling, th' East,
To wanton o'er that spicy nest.

Every tress must be confest,
But neatly tangled at the best;
Like a clew of golden thread
Most excellently ravellèd.

Do not then wind up that light
In ribbands, and o'ercloud in night,
Like the Sun in 's early ray;
But shake your head, and scatter day!

RICHARD LOVELACE 1618—58

$\mathcal{S}$PRING BEAUTY

Then we strolled on into the wood beyond the ash-meadow, and both of us sought for early primroses, and the fresh green crinkled leaves. She was not afraid of being alone with me after the first day. I never saw her so lovely, or so happy. I think she hardly knew why she was so happy all the time. I can see her now, standing under the budding branches of the gray trees, over which a tinge of green seemed to be deepening day after day, her sun-bonnet fallen back on her neck, her hands full of delicate wood-flowers, quite unconscious of my gaze, but intent on sweet mockery of some bird in neighbouring bush or tree. She had the art of warbling, and replying to the notes of different birds, and knew their song, their habits and ways, more accurately than any one else I ever knew. She had often done it at my request the spring before; but this year she really gurgled, and whistled, and warbled just as they did, out of the very fulness and joy of her heart.

Cousin Phillis, ELIZABETH GASKELL 1812–65

*G*O, LOVELY ROSE

Go, lovely Rose –
   Tell her that wastes her time and me,
   That now she knows,
When I resemble her to thee,
How sweet and fair she seems to be.

Tell her that's young,
And shuns to have her graces spied,
    That hadst thou sprung
In deserts where no men abide,
Thou must have uncommended died.

    Small is the worth
Of beauty from the light retired:
    Bid her come forth,
Suffer herself to be desired,
And not blush so to be admired.

    Then die – that she
The common fate of all things rare
    May read in thee;
How small a part of time they share
That are so wondrous sweet and fair!

EDMUND WALLER 1606–87

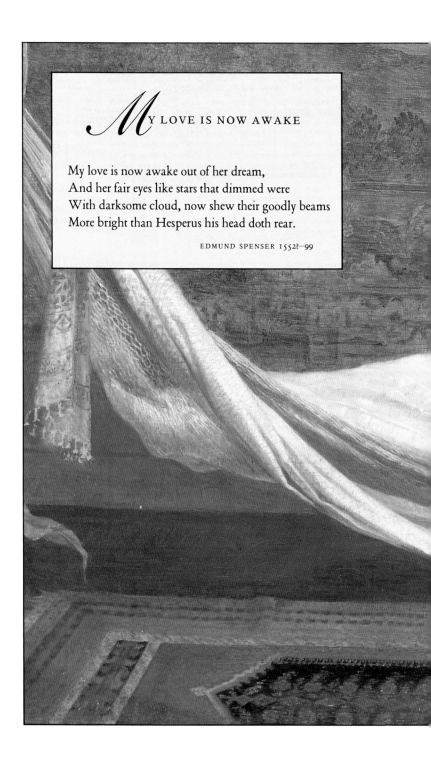

My Love Is Now Awake

My love is now awake out of her dream,
And her fair eyes like stars that dimmed were
With darksome cloud, now shew their goodly beams
More bright than Hesperus his head doth rear.

EDMUND SPENSER 1552?–99

ℐT IS NOT FLATTERY

Dear, simple girl, those flattering arts
From which thou'dst guard frail female hearts,
Exist but in imagination –
Mere phantoms of thine own creation:
For he who views that witching grace,
That perfect form, that lovely face,
With eyes admiring, oh! believe me,
He never wishes to deceive thee:
Once in thy polish'd mirror glance,
Thou'lt there descry that elegance
Which from our sex demand such praises,
But envy in the other raises:
Then he who tells thee of thy beauty,
Believe me, only does his duty:
Ah! fly not from the candid youth;
It is not flattery – 'tis truth.

GEORGE GORDON, LORD BYRON 1788–1824

$\mathcal{T}$HE ART OF DRESSING

She had the wonderful art of dressing to suit the season and the sky. To-day the art was ravishingly companionable with her sweet-lighted face: too sweet, too vividly meaningful for pretty, if not of the strict severity for beautiful. Millinery would tell us that she wore a fichu of thin white muslin crossed in front on a dress of the same light stuff, trimmed with deep rose. She carried a grey-silk parasol, traced at the borders with green creepers, and across the arm devoted to Crossjay a length of trailing ivy, and in that hand a bunch of the first long grasses. These hues of red rose and pale green ruffled and pouted in the billowy white of the dress ballooning and valleying softly, like a yacht before the sail bends low; but she walked not like one blown against; resembling rather the day of the South-west driving the clouds, gallantly firm in commotion; interfusing colour and varying in her features from laugh to smile and look of settled pleasure, like the heavens above the breeze.

The Egoist, GEORGE MEREDITH 1828–1909

*L*AURA SLEEPING

Winds, whisper gently whilst she sleeps,
    And fan her with your cooling wings;
Whilst she her drops of beauty weeps
    From pure and yet-unrivalled springs.

Glide over beauty's field, her face,
    To kiss her lip and cheek be bold,
But with a calm and stealing pace,
    Neither too rude, nor yet too cold.

Play in her beams, and crisp her hair,
　　With such a gale as wings soft love,
And with so sweet, so rich an air,
　　As breathes from the Arabian grove.

A breath as hushed as lover's sigh,
　　Or that unfolds the morning door;
Sweet as the winds that gently fly
　　To sweep the Spring's enamelled floor.

Murmur soft music to her dreams,
　　That pure and unpolluted run,
Like to the new-born crystal streams
　　Under the bright enamoured sun.

But when she waking shall display
　　Her light, retire within your bar:
Her breath is life, her eyes are day,
　　And all mankind her creatures are.

CHARLES COTTON 1630—87

My Wife

Trusty, dusky, vivid, true,
With eyes of gold and bramble-dew,
Steel true and blade-straight,
The great artificer
Made my mate.

Honour, anger, valour, fire,
A love that life could never tire,
Death quench or evil stir;
The mighty master
Gave to her.

Tender, tender, comrade, wife,
A fellow-farer true through life,
Heart-whole and soul-free,
The august father
Gave to me.

ROBERT LOUIS STEVENSON 1850–94

*S*HADOW OF YOUR BEAUTY

What is your substance, whereof are you made,
That millions of strange shadows on you tend?
Since every one hath, every one, one shade,
And you, but one, can every shadow lend.
Describe Adonis, and the counterfeit
Is poorly imitated after you;
On Helen's cheek all art of beauty set,
And you in Grecian tires are painted new:
Speak of the spring and foison of the year,
The one doth shadow of your beauty show,
The other as your bounty doth appear;
And you in every blessèd shape we know.
  In all external grace you have some part,
  But you like none, none you, for constant heart.

WILLIAM SHAKESPEARE 1564–1616

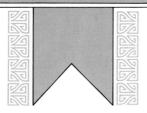

THE FAIR BUT CRUEL GIRL

The nymph that undoes me is fair and unkind,
No less than a wonder by nature designed;
She's the grief of my heart, but joy of my eye,
The cause of my flame, that never can die.
Her lips, from whence wit obligingly flows,
Have the colour of cherries and smell of the rose;
Love and destiny both attend on her will;
She saves with a smile, with a frown she can kill.
The desperate lover can hope no redress,
Where beauty and rigour are both in excess;
In Caelia they meet, so unhappy am I;
Who sees her must love; who loves her must die.

SIR GEORGE ETHEREGE ?1635–91

_S_HE WORE A NEW 'TERRA‑COTTA' DRESS

She wore a new 'terra‑cotta' dress,
And we stayed, because of the pelting storm,
Within the hansom's dry recess,
Though the horse had stopped; yea, motionless
   We sat on, snug and warm.

Then the downpour ceased, to my sharp sad pain
And the glass that had screened our forms before
Flew up, and out she sprang to her door:
I should have kissed her if the rain
   Had lasted a minute more.

THOMAS HARDY 1840–1928

$\mathcal{A}$WAKE

The lark now leaves his watery nest,
    And climbing shakes his dewy wings.
He takes this window for the East,
    And to implore your light he sings –
Awake, awake! the morn will never rise
Till she can dress her beauty at your eyes.

The merchant bows unto the seaman's star,
    The plowman from the sun his season takes;
But still the lover wonders what they are
    Who look for day before his mistress wakes.
Awake, awake! break through your veils of lawn!
Then draw your curtains, and begin the dawn!

WILLIAM DAVENANT 1606–68

MY LADY WALKS

My lady walks her morning round,
My lady's page her fleet greyhound,
My lady's hair the fond winds stir,
And all the birds make songs for her.

Her thrushes sing in Rathburn bowers,
And Rathburn side is gay with flowers;
But ne'er like hers, in flower or bird,
Was beauty seen or music heard.

Oh, proud and calm! — she cannot know
Where'er she goes with her I go;
Oh, cold and fair! — she cannot guess
I kneel to share her hound's caress!

The hound and I are on her trail,
The wind and I uplift her veil;
As if the calm, cold moon she were,
And I the tide, I follow her.

As unrebuked as they, I share
The licence of the sun and air,
And in a common homage hide
My worship from her scorn and pride.

No lance have I, in joust or fight,
To splinter in my lady's sight;
But, at her feet, how blest were I
For any need of hers to die!

JOHN GREENLEAF WHITTIER 1807–92

[61]

$\mathcal{A}$DMIRING PHILLIS

As we drew near the town, I could see some of the young fellows we met cast admiring looks on Phillis; and that made me look too. She had on a white gown, and a short black silk cloak, according to the fashion of the day. A straw bonnet with brown ribbon strings; that was all. But what her dress wanted in colour, her sweet bonny face had. The walk made her cheeks bloom like the rose; the very whites of her eyes had a blue tinge in them, and her dark eyelashes brought out the depth of the blue eyes themselves.

Cousin Phillis, ELIZABETH GASKELL 1812–65

$\mathcal{I}$N ADORATION

He placed himself at a corner of the door-way for her to pass him into the house, and doated on her cheek, her ear, and the softly dusky nape of her neck, where this way and that the little lighter-coloured irreclaimable curls running truant from the comb and the knot – curls, half-curls, root-curls, vine-ringlets, wedding-rings, fledgling feathers, tufts of down, blown wisps – waved or fell, waved over or up or involutedly, or strayed, loose and downward, in the form of small silken paws, hardly any of them much thicker than a crayon shading, cunninger than long round locks of gold to trick the heart.

The Egoist, GEORGE MEREDITH 1828–1909

To a Lady Admiring Herself in a Looking-Glass

Fair lady, when you see the grace
Of beauty in your looking-glass;
A stately forehead, smooth and high,
And full of princely majesty;
A sparkling eye, no gem so fair,
Whose lustre dims the Cyprian star;
A glorious cheek, divinely sweet,
Wherein both roses kindly meet;
A cherry lip that would entice
Even gods to kiss at any price;
You think no beauty is so rare
That with your shadow might compare;
That your reflection is alone
The thing that men most dote upon.
Madam, alas! your glass doth lie,
And you are much deceived; for I
A beauty know of richer grace —
Sweet, be not angry — 'tis your face.

THOMAS RANDOLPH 1605–35

My Lady's Presence

My lady's presence makes the roses red,
Because to see her lips they blush with shame.
The lily's leaves, for envy, pale became,
And her white hands in them this envy bred.
The marigold the leaves abroad did spread,
Because the sun's and her power is the same.
The violet of purple colour came,
Dyed in the blood she made my heart to shed.
In brief, all flowers from her their virtue take;
From her sweet breath their sweet smells do proceed;
The living heat which her eyebeams doth make
Warmeth the ground, and quickeneth the seed.
   The rain, wherewith she watereth the flowers,
    Falls from mine eyes, which she dissolves in showers.

HENRY CONSTABLE 1562–1613

[69]

*J*ULIET

I see you, Juliet, still, with your straw hat
Loaded with vines, and with your dear pale face,
On which those thirty years so lightly sat,
And the white outline of your muslin dress.
You wore a little *fichu* trimmed with lace
And crossed in front, as was the fashion then,
Bound at your waist with a broad band or sash,
All white and fresh and virginally plain.
There was a sound of shouting far away
Down in the valley, as they called to us,
And you, with hands clasped seeming still to pray
Patience of fate, stood listening to me thus
With heaving bosom. There a rose lay curled.
It was the reddest rose in all the world.

WILFRID BLUNT 1840–1922

A FAVOURITE PIECE

She immediately rose and went to the piano – a somewhat worn instrument that seemed to get the better of its infirmities under the firm touch of her small fingers as she preluded. Deronda placed himself where he could see her while she sang; and she took everything as quietly as if she had been a child going to breakfast.

Imagine her – it is always good to imagine a human creature in whom bodily loveliness seems as properly one with the entire being as the bodily loveliness of those wondrous transparent orbs of life that we find in the sea – imagine her with her dark hair brushed from her temples, but yet showing certain tiny rings there which had cunningly found their own way back, the mass of it hanging behind just to the nape of the little neck in curly fibres, such as renew themselves at their own will after being bathed into straightness like that of water-grasses. Then see the perfect cameo her profile makes, cut in a duskish shell where by some happy fortune there pierced a gem-like darkness for the eye and eyebrow; the delicate nostrils defined enough to be ready for sensitive movements, the finished ear, the firm curves of the chin and neck entering into the expression of a refinement which was not feebleness.

Daniel Deronda, GEORGE ELIOT 1819–80

AND WOULD YOU SEE MY MISTRESS' FACE

And would you see my mistress' face?
It is a flowery garden place
Where knots of beauties have such grace
That all is work and nowhere space.

It is a sweet delicious morn
Where day is breeding, never born.
It is a meadow yet unshorn
Which thousand flowers do adorn.

THOMAS CAMPION 1567–1619

VICTORIOUS BEAUTY

Victorious beauty, though your eyes
   Are able to subdue an hoast,
   And therefore are unlike to boast
The taking of a little prize,
Do not a single heart dispise.

It came alone, but yet so arm'd
   With former love, I durst have sworne
   That where a privy coat was worne,
With characters of beauty charm'd,
Thereby it might have scapt unharm'd.

But neither steel nor stony breast
   Are proofe against those lookes of thine,
   Nor can a Beauty lesse divine
Of any heart be long possest,
Where thou pretend'st an interest.

Thy Conquest in regard of me
   Alasse is small, but in respect
   Of her that did my Love protect,
Were it divulg'd, deserv'd to be
Recorded for a Victory.

And such a one, as some that view
   Her lovely face perhaps may say,
   Though you have stolen my heart away,
If all your servants prove not true,
May steale a heart or two from you.

AURELIAN TOWNSHEND 1583?–1651?

ℋER SIGHS TO SING

I saw my lady weep,
   And Sorrow proud to be advancèd so
In those fair eyes where all perfections keep.
   Her face was full of woe;
But such a woe, believe me, as wins more hearts
Than Mirth can do, with her enticing parts.

   Sorrow was there made fair,
   And passion wise, tears a delightful thing,
Silence beyond all speech a wisdom rare.
   She made her sighs to sing,
And all things with so sweet a sadness move,
As made my heart at once both grieve and love.

   O fairer than aught else
The world can show! Leave off in time to grieve.
Enough, enough! Your joyful looks excels:
   Tears kills the heart, believe.
   O strive not to be excellent in woe,
Which only breeds your beauty's overthrow.

ANONYMOUS SEVENTEENTH CENTURY

A PERFECT LADY

Gwendolen was already mounted and riding up and down the avenue when Rex appeared at the gate. She had provided herself against disappointment in case he did not appear in time by having the groom ready behind her, for she would not have waited beyond a reasonable time. But now the groom was dismissed, and the two rode away in delightful freedom. Gwendolen was in her highest spirits, and Rex thought that she had never looked so lovely before: her figure, her long white throat, and the curves of her cheek and chin were always set off to perfection by the compact simplicity of her riding dress. He could not conceive a more perfect girl; and to a youthful lover like Rex it seems that the fundamental identity of the good, the true, and the beautiful, is already extant and manifest in the object of his love.

Daniel Deronda, GEORGE ELIOT 1819–80

THY SWEET VOICE

There be none of Beauty's daughters
    With a magic like thee;
And like music on the waters
    Is thy sweet voice to me:
When, as if its sound were causing
The charmed ocean's pausing,
The waves lie still and gleaming,
And the lull'd winds seem dreaming:

And the midnight moon is weaving
    Her bright chain o'er the deep;
Whose breast is gently heaving,
    As an infant's asleep:
So the spirit bows before thee,
To listen and adore thee;
With a full but soft emotion,
Like the swell of Summer's ocean

GEORGE GORDON, LORD BYRON 1788–1824

[82]

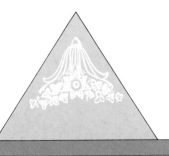

A DAMSEL

A damsel with a dulcimer
In a vision once I saw:
It was an Abyssinian maid,
And on her dulcimer she played,
Singing of Mount Abora.
Could I revive within me
Her symphony and song,
To such a deep delight 'twould win me,
That with music loud and long.

SAMUEL TAYLOR COLERIDGE 1772–1834

$\mathcal{S}$LEEP, MY BEAUTY

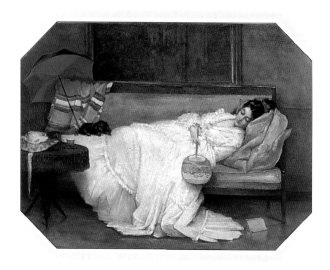

Sleep, angry beauty, sleep, and fear not me.
For who a sleeping lion dares provoke?
It shall suffice me here to sit and see
Those lips shut up that never kindly spoke.
    What sight can more content a lover's mind
    Than beauty seeming harmless, if not kind?

My words have charmed her, for secure she sleeps;
Though guilty of much wrong done to my love;
And in her slumber, see, she close-eyed weeps:
Dreams often more than waking passions move.
    Plead, sleep, my cause; and make her soft like thee,
    That she in peace may wake and pity me.

THOMAS CAMPION 1567–1619

A POSY FOR LAURA

Come, ye fair ambrosial flowers,
Leave your beds and leave your bowers,
Blooming, beautiful, and rare,
Form a posy for my Fair;
Fair and bright and blooming be,
Meet for such a Nymph as she.
Let the young vermilion rose
A becoming blush disclose,
Such as Laura's cheeks display,
When she steals my heart away.

FRANCIS FAWKES 1720–77

*S*OUL'S BEAUTY

Under the arch of Life, where love and death,
    Terror and mystery, guard her shrine, I saw
   Beauty enthroned; and though her gaze struck awe,
I drew it in as simply as my breath.
Hers are the eyes which, over and beneath,
    The sky and sea bend on thee, – which can draw,
   By sea or sky or woman, to one law,
The allotted bondman of her palm and wreath.

This is that Lady Beauty, in whose praise
    Thy voice and hand shake still, – long known to thee
      By flying hair and fluttering hem, – the beat
      Following her daily of thy heart and feet,
   How passionately and irretrievably,
In what fond flight, how many ways and days!

DANTE GABRIEL ROSSETTI 1828–82

Stanzas to Lady Wilmot Horton

She walks in beauty, like the night
    Of cloudless climes and starry skies;
And all that's best of dark and bright
    Meet in her aspect and her eyes:
Thus mellowed to that tender light
    Which heaven to gaudy day denies.

One shade the more, one ray the less,
    Had half impaired the nameless grace
Which waves in every raven tress,
    Or softly lightens o'er her face;
Where thoughts serenely sweet express
    How pure, how dear their dwelling-place.

And on that cheek, and o'er that brow,
    So soft, so calm, yet eloquent,
The smiles that win, the tints that glow,
    But tell of days in goodness spent,
A mind at peace with all below,
    A heart whose love is innocent!

GEORGE GORDON, LORD BYRON 1788–1824

LIST OF PAINTINGS

Slipcase and Frontispiece: *Lady Agnew of Lochnaw*, J. S. Sargent;
p. 4 19th C. Valentine Card; pp. 6–7 *Ask Me No More*, L. Alma-
Tadema; p. 8 *The Flower Seller*, W. Powell Frith; p. 11 *The Rose
From Armida's Garden*, M. Stillman; p. 12 *Portrait of Miss Dorothy
Dicksee*, F. Dicksee; p. 14 *A Tea Party in the Garden*, A. Oliver;
p. 15 *Golden Curls* (detail), C. S. Lidderdale; p. 17 *Portrait of Mrs
Kathleen Newton*, J. J. J. Tissot; p. 18 *An English Rose*, E. Vernon;
p. 20 *Jeannie on the Rocks*, J. H. Gunn; p. 22 *Lady Palmer*,
F. Dicksee; p. 25 *The Artist and his Model*, J. Ballantyne; p. 26
A Fair Maid, H. Ryland; p. 29 *Shimmering Summer*, A. Hacker;
p. 30 *Portrait of a Lady said to be Anna de Noailles* (detail), H. D.
Etcheverry; p. 31 *Still Life with Roses and Pansies*, J. L. Jensen; p. 32
Louis – The Blue Jacket, W. de Glehn; p. 35 *Picking Roses*,
E. Vernon; p. 36 *Profile of a Young Girl* (detail), A. Maillol; p. 37
Still Life of Peach Roses, A. Dubrus; p. 38 *Gabriel D'Estress*,
W. Powell Frith; p. 41 *Elegant Figure*, H. Rae; p. 42 *Marguerite*
(detail), E. Vernon; pp. 44–5 *Young Girl in White Satin Dress*,
J. Everett Millais; p. 46 *A Lady Looking in a Mirror by an Open Door*,
C. Holsoe; p. 49 *Woman with Parasol Turned Right*, C. Monet; p. 50
Slumber, I. Snowman; p. 53 *Portrait of Lady Sutherland*, E. A. Ward;
p. 54 *Christobel finds Geraldine*, W. G. Collingwood; p. 56 *The
Arrival* (detail), E. Killingworth Johnson; p. 57 *Dressing Up*,
C. E. Perugini; p. 59 *At The Window*, A. Alma-Tadema; p. 60
Diana of the Uplands, C. W. Furse; pp. 62–3 *A Summer Garden*,
F. Toussaint; p. 65 *The Letter* (detail), B. Kaufmann; p. 66 *An
Invitation to the Opera*, H. J. Burgers; p. 68 *End of the Story*, M. Stone,
p. 69 *Peonies and Roses*, M. Lemaire; p. 71 *Poppy Girl*, S. P.
Kendrick; p. 72 *A Favourite Piece*, R. de Madrazo; pp. 74–5
Gathering Wild Flowers, A. Glendening; p. 77 *The Evening Shawl*,
A. Barnes; p. 79 *Portrait of a Young Woman*, E. F. Aman-Jean; p. 80
Le Chapeau Bleu (detail), C. S. Lidderdale; p. 83 *The Forgotten
Melody*, E. Walker; p. 84 *Chant d'Amour* (detail), E. Burne-Jones;
p. 86 *Girl with a Japanese Fan Asleep on a Sofa*, A. Stevens; p. 89
Falling Leaves, J. M. Strudwick; p. 90 *A Beauty*, E. de Blaas.

Anonymous *I saw my lady weep* p. 78. Wilfrid Blunt *Farewell to Juliet* p. 70. John Byrom, from *Colin and Phebe, A Pastoral* p. 37. Lord George Gordon Byron, To Miss— p. 47; *There be none of Beauty's daughters* p. 82; *Stanzas to Lady Wilmot Horton* p. 90. Thomas Campion, *And would you see my mistress' face?* p. 74; *Sleep, Angry Beauty* p. 86 Samuel Taylor Coleridge, from *Kubla Khan* p. 85. Henry Constable, *My lady's presence makes the roses red* p. 69. Thomas Carew, *A Song* p. 18. Charles Cotton, *Laura Sleeping* p. 50. William Davenant *Song* p. 58. Henry Austin Dobson, *Urceus Exit; Triolet* p. 36. George Eliot, from *Daniel Deronda* p. 73 and p. 80. Sir George Etherege *The Fair but cruel Girl* p. 56. Francis Fawkes, *A Nosegay for Laura* p. 87. Michael Field, *La Gioconda, by Leonardo Da Vinci, in the Louvre* p. 10. Elizabeth Gaskell, from *Cousin Phillis* p. 40 and p. 63. Thomas Hardy, from *The Return of the Native* p. 16; from *Tess of the D'Urbervilles* p. 34; *She wore a new 'terra-cotta' dress* p. 57. Thomas Hood, *Ruth* p. 28. Thomas Lodge, *For Pity, Pretty Eyes, Surcease* p. 9. Richard Lovelace *To Amarantha, that she would dishevel her hair* p. 39. George Meredith from *The Egoist* p. 48 and p. 64. Thomas Otway, *The Enchantment* p. 33. Thomas Randolph, *To a lady admiring herself in a looking-glass* p. 67. Dante Gabriel Rossetti, *Soul's Beauty* p. 88. William Shakespeare, *O, how much more doth beauty beauteous seem* p. 14; *The forward violet thus did I chide* p. 31; *What is your substance, whereof are you made?* p. 55. Spenser Edmund *The glorious portrait of that Angel's face* p. 25; from *Epithalamion* p. 44. Robert Louis Stevenson, *Thy Wife* p. 52. Joshua Sylvester, *Sweet mouth, that send'st a musky-rosed breath* p. 15. Lord Alfred Tennyson, *O Beauty* p. 7; from *Rosalind* p. 21; from *Eleänore* p. 23; from *A Dream of Fair Women* p. 27; from *Madeline* p. 30. Aurelian Townshend, *Victorious beauty, through your eyes* p. 76. Edmund Waller, *Go, lovely Rose* p. 42. John Greenleaf Whittier, *The Henchman* p. 60.

PICTURE ACKNOWLEDGEMENTS

The publishers wish to thank the following for permission to reproduce the illustrations: Bridgeman Art Library, London, with acknowledgements to: Private Collections pp. 6–7, 17, 44–5; Guildhall Art Gallery, London p. 8; Bonhams, London p. 11; Colnaghi, London p. 12; Roy Miles Fine Paintings, London p. 22; Christopher Wood Gallery, London pp. 25, 53, 59; Musée Huacinthe Rigaud, Perpignan p. 36; Musée D'Orsay, Paris p. 49; Musée du Petit Palais, Paris p. 79; Metropolitan Museum of Art, New York p. 84. Christie's Colour Library, London pp. 30, 31, 46, 86, 87, 89. Mary Evans Picture Library, London p. 4. Fine Art Photographic Library, London pp. 14, 15, 18, 26, 29, 35, 38, 41, 42, 50, 54, 56, 57, 62–3, 65, 66, 68, 69, 71, 72, 74–5, 80, 90. Laing Art Gallery, Newcastle upon Tyne (Tyne and Wear Museums Service) p. 83. Photographs by courtesy of David Messum Fine Paintings, London W1 pp. 20, 32, 37, 77. National Gallery of Scotland: Slipcase and Frontispiece. Tate Gallery, London p. 60.

DEAR FRIEND, FOR YOUR PLEASURE
THE PAGES OF THIS TREASURY
OF ROMANTIC VERSE HAVE BEEN
SPECIALLY SCENTED WITH THE
BEAUTIFUL FRAGRANCE
OF VICTORIA, THE SIGNATURE
PERFUME OF VICTORIA'S SECRET.

*V*ICTORIA

CONCEIVED AND DESIGNED
IN LONDON
BY VICTORIA'S SECRET

Selection copyright © Victoria's Secret and
George Weidenfeld & Nicolson Ltd, London 1990

First published in 1990
by Victoria's Secret,
10 Margaret Street, London WIN 7LF and
George Weidenfeld & Nicolson Ltd,
91 Clapham High Street, London SW4 7TA

Text selected by Barbara Mellor
Picture research by Juliet Brightmore

Printed and bound in Italy